Through My Eyes

DONNA PELLECCHIA

Presentation by *BookLeaf Publishing*

Web: www.bookleafpub.com

E-mail: info@bookleafpub.com

ISBN: 9789395087124

First edition 2022

DEDICATION

For my babies, mummy loves you all.

ACKNOWLEDGEMENT

Massive love to my biggest fans, the three humans I created, grew inside me and have raised singlehandedly to the best of my ability. Thank you to Dan & Tracy for encouraging me to write a book. They've been doing this for years! Well, guys, here it is!
Thank you to my manfriend, my lover, my swain. You didn't want a mention but you're getting one anyway because you have my back and are cheering me on!

PREFACE

One of my lifetime ambitions is to have my written work published. I was constantly writing stories as a child and teenager.

A few years ago i decided to take the plunge and write a book, although I always let my insecurities take over and so I never did it...until now!

After A' Levels I studied journalism and had a few pieces published in student magazines and the local football club's matchday programmes.

The Ones I Couldn't Hold

Nobody knew you were there,
But me
We had seven short weeks
And a life of what might have beens,
With every rotation of the sun
Those dates appear again,
I think where you'd be
And what we'd do,
I know your souls live on
But your bodies never did,
Nothing changes the fact I'm still your mum,
The three babies
I couldn't hold.

Version Of Me

You thought I'd be sad without your presence
I'm the best version of me,
Without your restraints.
I was your project,
Your toy,
Your puppet.
Manipulation and deceit
Was all you ever gave me
Oh, and the occasional broken jawbone,
Ripped clothes and smashed phone.
You never deserved me,
I'm better than you.
You didn't break me,
You gave my love the best version of me.

For My Grandparents

The flowers didn't bloom
The sun didn't shine
Was a grey and bleak time
I was lonely
I cried
I didn't resist self destruction
I drank
I blotted out the grief
Sought therapy
Battled emotions
They won the fight
I was exhausted from the nightmare
I knew you would leave
You told me when I was young
I just didn't want to hear the truth
Your body couldn't take any more
You were ready for your wings
I know you're watching
And I hope I make you proud
Don't forget me, grandparents
Meet me when it's my turn

Tales

I travel without exiting
From my safe confines,
Watching without eyes,
Listening without ears.
I experience without being
You speak to me,
Teach me,
Touch me,
Invoke emotion,
No limit of time and place.
Made of tree
Though you are not wood,
You leave memories
In my mind
Like printed words on paper,
Or paint upon a wall

Fibromyalgia

Like birth pains in my legs
And arms too heavy to lift
I'm tired
Not tired, exhausted
Can't stop eating
Don't want to eat
Can't remember my name
Did I take my pills?
I need to sleep
But I'm in too much agony
It hurts
I cry
I laugh
I laugh when I'm in pain
Humour is my coping mechanism
But it hurts too much
To giggle
To sit
To stand
To lay
To look
To hear
The lights are too bright
The birdsong, too loud

Every inch of my body expands
Swells in the flare
My eyelashes are heavy
Lids won't stay open
My brain is hot
Rolling in my skull
Like dice on a board game
Did I take my meds?
How long this will last
Is not for me to speculate
I can only hope it passes soon
My skeleton wants to escape
My muscles are clenching
Holding the bones tight
My nerves are on the brink
Everything hurts, aches
Stabbing pains
Contracting pains
Breathe through the pain
Did I take my meds?
My muscles are twitching
Involuntary spasms
Grateful to be introvert
If I was outside, I'd look deranged
My body fighting with itself
Did I even take my meds?

Music

Beats, riffs, rhythm
Melody
Harmonies feed my soul
Ignite the fire
Euphoria climbing higher
Lyrics repeat in my mind
Words live on
The legacy of those passed
Deep as the ocean
Shallow like a puddle
Speaking to different emotions
Within my being
Happy, elated, energised
Sad, angry, relaxed
All along the watchtower
A staircase to Heaven
The highway to Hell
The gambler in a ring of fire
Independent women
Are drunk in love
I am
I feel
When I hear music
I'm like a champagne supernova
In the sky

Springtime

Buttercups and daisies
Tulips and daffs
Chicks and lambs
A new season born
The celestial body
Grows bigger to the eye
Brighter and brighter
She glows in the sky
Clover in the meadows
Forget-me-nots
Bluebells
No longer a coat required
A cardi will suffice
Spring is here
Aries illuminated by the sun
The pink cherry blossom tree
Blooms increasingly every day
Colours more vibrant
Leaves turning greener
Mood of the masses, happier
We change what we eat
Banished are the stews
Bring out the salad
Away goes the brandy,
Crack open the Pimms!

Springtime is here
Embrace new beginnings
Rejoice in the vibrancy
Lighter evenings and warm nights

Barbeque Lullaby

If all the raindrops
Were spare ribs
And pork chops
Oh!
What a rain that
Would be!
I'd go outside
With my salad and
My plate
I wouldn't care
If I went to bed
Real late
If all the raindrops
Were spare ribs
And pork chops
Oh!
What a rain
That would be!

One

Jovial like succeeding generations
Confabulate like consorts
Osculate like striplings
Copulate like paramour
No other exists
Two pieces
Of the same puzzle
Both sides
Of the same coin
"We" and "Us"
From the inception
Until beyond every culmination
There will be "Us" and "We"
Eternally
We were two
Transformed into one

Writer's Block

I want to write
But my mind goes blank
I think of words
But I can't think of any words
I feel illiterate
I know I can
I have people cheering me on
Come on!
Write your book
Write a poem
Poems don't have to rhyme
Just let it flow
Random words
Pop into my mind
Wall
Show
Cup
Shelf
Book
Drawer
Text
Boat
Ship
River
Space

Can
Journal
Earring
It's no good,
I can't call that poetry
What would John and William do?
Have a cup of tea and a walk
Well I'm not keen on tea
And I'm suppose to be at work
So the walk and wait
Ooh!
Walk.
I must walk to the shop
To purchase dancing juice
For tomorrow's shenanigans
My birthday party
Twenty-one with twenty years experience
Wouldn't want to go back to my twenties
Wasn't the best of times
Oh, Lord, I'm rambling now
Someone shut me up!

Customer Service

I am not your verbal punchbag
You want my help
I am doing my job
I am not the company
I want to help
I could cancel your transaction
I could block your refund
I don't earn enough
To be your verbal punchbag
So your wardrobe has been delayed
No one died,
You're still alive!
So you live forty miles
From the nearest store,
Shop closer to home.
Accept if you have to wait,
So do many others.
I'm at work,
I'm not here for you to shout at.
I didn't change your delivery date
Although I could...
You want my help
Because it's my job
Use the tone and language
You want me to use.

You sold your sofa
Before the new one arrived
That's not my fault
You did that, your choice
I can't say this to you
Because...
"Customer"

My Choice

I wish you could stay,
But that would be
No good for you
I'm sorry, my baby
This is the best for you.
If I keep you
It would be unfair,
You'd have no independence,
No playing in the park.
You'd have no
Knowledge or awareness
Of us, and things, around you.
Mummy's health conditions
Would impact you endlessly.
You'd be as an addict's,
And that's far from you deserve.
Believe me,
Mummy and daddy love you dearly
And this is why
I have to set your soul free
And when you are embodied,
We'll meet howbeit time is ready

Love

Lounging in our pyjamas
Occasionally napping during films
Vehemently taking care of one another
Every moment, not being taken for granted
Evidently we were made for each other
Viciously sharing private jokes
Our relationship holds many levels
L'amour toujours

Charlie

You're the one
That made me a mother.
My firstborn,
My first love,
My friend.
You saved me from self destruction
And you pushed me to the brink.
When you were in a dark place,
I helped you find the light.
I taught you to read, write,
And use cutlery,
I wiped your bum.
Fought doctors,
Psychiatrists,
Audiologists,
Teachers and relatives
For you and with you.
I probably could have done better,
But you never went without.
Always had love, shelter, warmth
And a full belly.
You taught me many things too,
I could never be without you.
I loved you as soon as those
Lines of blue appeared.

And no matter what you do,
Mummy will always
Love you, Choo

Irrelevant

There was a time
When I thought we were mates
And then you did me wrong
Took me for a twat
Until I realised
And took those metaphorical scissors
And snip, snip, snipped
Now I know the irrelevant
Are probably not reading this,
So I don't need to get personal
Some people became irrelevant
Because I saw them for what they were.
That nicey-nicey attitude only lasted so long
Until your mask dropped
And true colours surfaced
Your backhanded compliments
And condescending comments
Soon remodelled as abhorrent
And then I realised
You're just insigificunt!

Yoghurt

I once wrote about yoghurt
Which seems as crazy as
Eric & Ernie
Two-hundred and fifty words
I was definitely heard
As twenty years later
People still mention
My tribute to a
Muller-Light Corner

21st Century Dating

Online dating is a full time job
Except you're paid
With crappy chat-up lines
And spammed with photos
You didn't ask for...
And could live without!
Be specific with your requirements
And stay in control
Who are these blokes, anyway?
Gym selfies
Fish handlers
The ugly ones always post group pics
And why do they show us their kids?!
You tell them what you want
A relationship
And they tell you the same
So you chat for a while,
A date or two,
And then they do their best
Impression of Casper
And ghost you.
Whaaaaat?!
And then everyone says,
"You'll meet The One soon"
And you say,

"How, when they're all arsehole-fuckwits?"
You delete the app,
You get bored and try again
Eat, sleep, swipe left, repeat
And then you notice
One profile that keeps popping up
When you've swiped left
Five times, you think,
"Sod it! Why not?"
You talk,
You meet,
And it turns out,
He's The One!

Teen Text

Kids sending messages in code
Or at least they think it's code!
Twas Gen X that created this code,
On our Nokia 3310s
We had ten texts a day
And only a few characters
To get all info across
Our messages read:

R U OK WUU2? PUB @ 12. TBLY

YH OK TBLY2

Now these kids have unlimited texts
And unlimited characters,
And the messages still read

WUU2

NUTIN STL U

NUTIN WYS

RAH

U C DAT PENG TING

IDGAFS BRUH

FR

RAH

KK SAY NUTIN

You have unlimited texts, data and calls
And you say NUTIN?